# REAL WORLD DATA

# GRAPHING THE UNIVERSE

Deborah Underwood

Heinemann
LIBRARY

**H www.heinemann.co.uk/library**
Visit our website to find out more information about **Heinemann Library** books.

To order:
☎ Phone 44 (0) 1865 888066
📄 Send a fax to 44 (0) 1865 314091
💻 Visit the Heinemann Bookshop at www.heinemann.co.uk/library to browse our catalogue and order online.

Heinemann Library is an imprint of Pearson Education Limited, a company incorporated in England and Wales having its registered office at Edinburgh Gate, Harlow, Essex, CM20 2JE – Registered company number: 00872828
Heinemann Library is a registered trademark of Pearson Education Limited
Text © Pearson Education Ltd 2009
First published in hardback in 2009
First published in paperback in 2009
The moral rights of the proprietor have been asserted.

Edited by Nancy Dickmann, Rachel Howells, and Sian Smith
Designed by Victoria Bevan and Geoff Ward
Illustrated by Geoff Ward
Picture Research by Mica Brancic and Elaine Willis
Originated by Modern Age
Printed and bound in China by Leo Paper Group

13-digit ISBN 978 0 431 02947 4 (hardback)
13 12 11 10 09
10 9 8 7 6 5 4 3 2 1

13-digit ISBN 978 0 431 02961 0 (paperback)
13 12 11 10 09
10 9 8 7 6 5 4 3 2 1

**British Library Cataloguing in Publication Data**
Underwood, Deborah
Graphing the universe. - (Real world data)
523.1'0728

A full catalogue record for this book is available from the British Library.

**Acknowledgements**
The publishers would like to thank the following for permission to reproduce photographs:
© Jerry Lodriguss (Science Photo Library) p.**21**; © Jon Lomberg (Science Photo Library) p.**19 left**; © Mark Garlick (Science Photo Library) p.**9**; © Mehau Kulyk (Science Photo Library) p.**4**; © NASA pp.**6**, **16**, **25**, **26**, **5** (Corbis, STScI), **11**, **12**, **14**, **15** (Science Photo Library), **23** (H. Ford (JHU), G. Illingworth (UCSC/LO), M.Clampin (STScI), G. Hartig (STScI), the ACS Science Team, and ESA); © Science Photo Library p.**19 right**

Cover photograph of Crab Nebula, reproduced with permission of ©Corbis (NASA, STScI).

Every effort has been made to contact copyright holders of any material reproduced in this book. Any omissions will be rectified in subsequent printings if notice is given to the publishers.

The publishers would like to thank Harold Pratt for his assistance in the preparation of this book.

**Disclaimer**
All the Internet addresses (URLs) given in this book were valid at time of going to press. However, due to the dynamic nature of the Internet, some addresses may have changed, or sites may have changed or ceased to exist since publication. While the author and publishers regret any inconvenience this may cause readers, no responsibility for any such changes can be accepted by either the author or the publishers. It is recommended that adults supervise children on the Internet.

# CONTENTS

Some words are printed in bold, **like this**. You can find out what they mean by looking in the glossary, on page 30.

If you go outside on a clear night, you may see the Moon shining in the sky. You may also see a steady glow coming from **planets** such as Venus and Mars. The Moon and planets shine because they reflect light from our closest star, the Sun.

Our **solar system** is made up of the Sun and everything that **orbits** it. This includes the Earth, the Moon, other planets, and their **satellites**. It also includes some other space objects, such as **comets** and **asteroids**.

The solar system is part of the Milky Way **galaxy**. A galaxy is a collection of stars, dust, and gases. Far past the Milky Way, billions of other galaxies spin in space. The universe is made up of our galaxy, other galaxies, and everything around them.

## Space science

**Astronomy** is the study of space and the objects it holds. Astronomers collect and study **data**, or information, about space. Because of their work, we know a lot about the universe.

### Large distances

The distance between the Sun and the Earth is about 150 million kilometres (93 million miles). This distance is also known as one **astronomical unit**, or AU. Astronomical units help astronomers talk easily about large distances. For example, Jupiter is about 5 AU from the Sun. This makes it clear that Jupiter is five times further from the Sun than the Earth is.

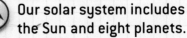 Our solar system includes the Sun and eight planets.

This photograph shows some of the galaxies that make up the universe.

# Graphs and charts

An astronomer may organize data by putting it into a table. Data can also be turned into a graph. A graph is a picture that shows information. These pictures make it easy to compare data. This table (right) shows the distances between the Sun and each planet in Astronomical Units. The bar chart below shows the same information. Which is easier to understand?

| Planet | Distance from the Sun in astronomical units (AU) |
|--------|------------------------------------------------|
| Mercury | 0.4 |
| Venus | 0.7 |
| Earth | 1 |
| Mars | 1.5 |
| Jupiter | 5.2 |
| Saturn | 9.5 |
| Uranus | 19.2 |
| Neptune | 30.1 |

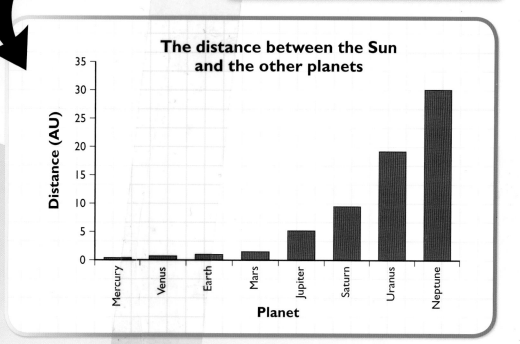

The distance between the Sun and the other planets

# THE SUN

Like other stars, the Sun is a ball of burning gases. The Sun is mostly made of hydrogen and helium. As the hydrogen burns, the Sun gives off heat and light. The temperature in the centre of the Sun is about 15,000,000 °C (27,000,000 °F). The highest temperature ever recorded in one of Africa's scorching deserts was only 57.8 °C (136 °F)!

The Sun's light and warmth make life on Earth possible. Without the Sun, the Earth would be too cold for life as we know it to survive. Plants need sunlight to make food. This food is used by plants and by the animals that eat them.

## The Sun's strong pull

The Sun contains nearly all the **mass** in the **solar system**. Mass is the amount of **matter** in any object. The more mass an object has, the stronger its **gravity**. This means the more it pulls other objects towards it. The Sun has the strongest gravity of anything in the solar system. That is why **planets** and other objects in the solar system **orbit** the Sun.

The Sun's surface can be very active, shooting material into space like a fiery fountain.

## Light years

A **light year** might sound like a way to measure time. It is actually a way to measure distance. A light year is the distance that light travels in one year. Light travels very quickly – 299,792 kilometres (186,282 miles) per second! Distances in space are huge. Which is simpler: to say a certain star is 8 light years away, or to say it is 75,634,039,643,904 kilometres (46,996,813,387,258 miles) away?

## Pie charts

Pie charts show the parts that make up a whole. This chart shows the gases that make up the Sun. A **key** shows which colour represents each gas. The chart makes it easy to see that the Sun contains more hydrogen than helium.

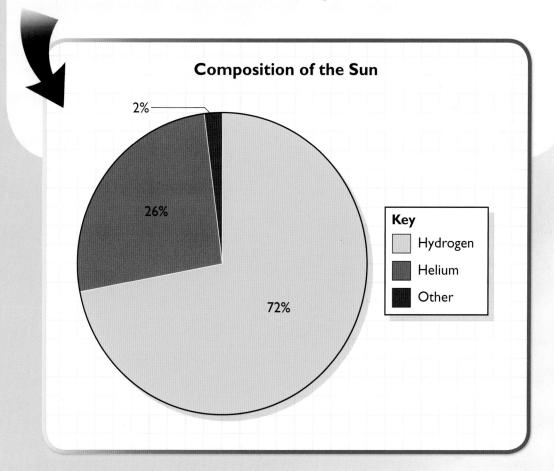

**Composition of the Sun**

2%

26%

72%

**Key**
- Hydrogen
- Helium
- Other

**Planets** are large round objects that **orbit** stars. In our **solar system**, eight planets orbit the Sun. Each takes a different amount of time to make the trip. The time a planet takes to orbit the Sun determines how long the planet's year is. The Earth takes 365 days to orbit the Sun, so our year is 365 days long.

Each planet **rotates**, or spins, on its **axis**. The axis is an imaginary line that runs through the planet. The amount of time the planet takes to spin around once is the length of its day. An Earth day is 24 hours. Venus rotates much more slowly. Its day is 243 Earth days long!

## Weight on other worlds

Different planets and stars have different **masses**. The greater a planet's mass, the greater the pull of its **gravity**. Weight measures how much gravity is pulling an object. This means that your weight changes depending on where you are. If you weigh 45 kilograms (100 pounds) on the Earth, you would only weigh 8 kilograms (17 pounds) on the Moon. But you would weigh 115 kilograms (253 pounds) on Jupiter!

## Graphing data

This table shows the length of the day and the year on each planet. It would be hard to graph this **data**, because some of the numbers are so small and others so large.

| Planet | Length of day in Earth days | Length of year in Earth years |
|--------|------------------------------|-------------------------------|
| Mercury | 58.6 | 0.2 |
| Venus | 243 | 0.6 |
| Earth | 1 | 1 |
| Mars | 1 | 1.9 |
| Jupiter | 0.4 | 11.9 |
| Saturn | 0.4 | 29.4 |
| Uranus | 0.7 | 84 |
| Neptune | 0.7 | 164.8 |

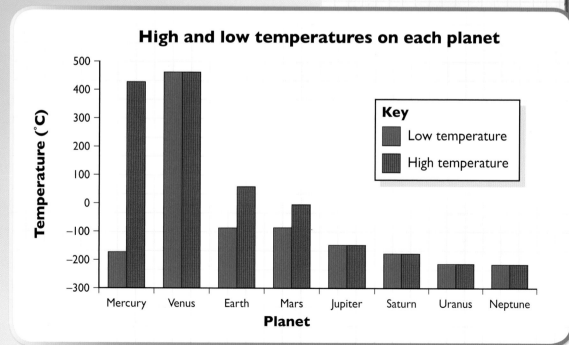

▲ Planets vary greatly in size, as this picture shows.

# Layers of gases

An **atmosphere**, or layer of gases, surrounds each planet. Mercury's atmosphere is very thin. Venus has the thickest atmosphere in the solar system. Atmosphere plays a role in a planet's temperature. A thicker atmosphere will trap more heat. A planet's temperature also depends on how far the planet is from the Sun.

▼ A double bar chart uses bars to show two sets of data. This graph compares low and high temperatures for each planet.

## High and low temperatures on each planet

**Temperature (°C)**

500
400
300
200
100
0
-100
-200
-300

**Key**
■ Low temperature
■ High temperature

Mercury　Venus　Earth　Mars　Jupiter　Saturn　Uranus　Neptune

**Planet**

# THE ROCKY PLANETS

Mercury, Venus, Earth, and Mars are the four **planets** closest to the Sun. They are sometimes called the rocky planets because they are made mostly of rocks.

The planet Mercury is the smallest planet, and the closest planet to the Sun. It has the widest temperature range of any planet. During the day, the temperature can reach 427 °C (801 °F). At night, it can drop to as low as -173 °C (-279 °F).

## Line graphs

Line graphs often show how something changes over time. Time is usually shown on the **x-axis**. Mercury has an oval-shaped **orbit**. This line graph shows that sometimes Mercury is much closer to the Sun than other times.

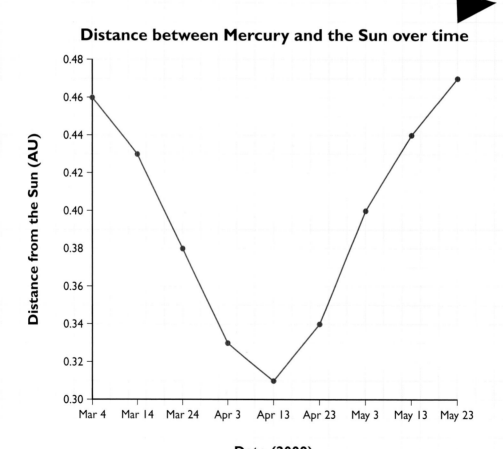

**Distance between Mercury and the Sun over time**

*Date (2009)*

Venus's thick **atmosphere** traps a lot of heat. The average temperature on the surface is 462 °C (864 °F). Venus is even hotter than Mercury, even though it is further from the Sun.

Earth is the only planet that we know supports life. Its temperature allows liquid water to exist. If it were further from the Sun, the water might freeze. If it were closer, the water might evaporate (turn into a gas).

Mars is sometimes called the red planet. Iron-rich minerals in the soil on Mars give the planet its red-orange colour. There are ice caps near the poles on Mars, just as there are on the Earth.

Venus shines brightly in the night sky because its thick atmosphere reflects lots of sunlight.

## Parts of a graph

The x-axis is the horizontal line that usually goes across the bottom of a graph. The **y-axis** is the vertical line that is usually on the left side. Labels tell us what **data** each axis shows. This bar chart compares the diameters of the rocky planets. The planets are shown on the x-axis. The y-axis shows their diameters.

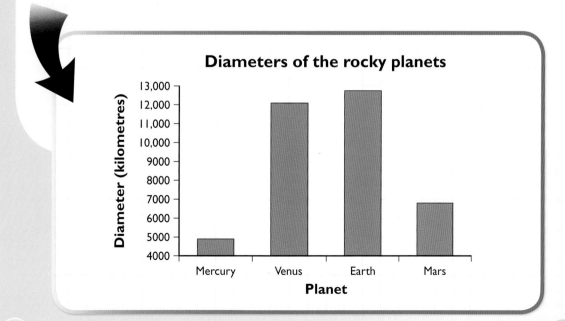

# THE GAS GIANTS

Jupiter, Saturn, Uranus, and Neptune are known as the **solar system's** gas giants. Unlike the rocky **planets**, the gas giant planets do not have solid surfaces. A spaceship would not be able to land on them. Instead, the outer layers of the planets are made of gases and liquids. The planets' centres, or cores, are probably made of rock or rock and ice.

Jupiter is the largest planet in the solar system. Its **mass** is about 318 times the mass of Earth. Jupiter **rotates** more quickly than any other planet in the solar system – its day is less than 10 Earth hours long.

## What's in a name?

The names of all the planets except Earth come from Greek and Roman myths (stories). For instance, in Roman myths, Jupiter was the king of the gods.

Jupiter's Great Red Spot is actually a huge swirling storm.

12

Saturn is the second-largest planet, but it is lighter than water. If Saturn were dropped into an enormous ocean, it would float! All the gas giants are circled by rings, but the rings around Saturn are the brightest. Saturn's rings are mostly made of ice.

Uranus and Neptune are the outermost planets. Blue-green Uranus has an **axis** that is quite tilted. Instead of spinning around like a globe, Uranus rolls like a bead on a string. Neptune's winds are the strongest in the solar system. They can blow at speeds of 2,000 kilometres (1,243 miles) per hour. On Earth, winds of 119 kilometres (74 miles) per hour are considered hurricane-force.

## Size and scale

Compare this graph to the graph on page 11. At first glance, you might think that the gas giants are smaller than the rocky planets. But look closely at the labels and numbers on the left of the graphs. You'll see that the **scales** of the graphs are different. The numbers on the **y-axis** of the graph below are in thousands of kilometres. So "80" stands for 80 thousand kilometres (80,000).

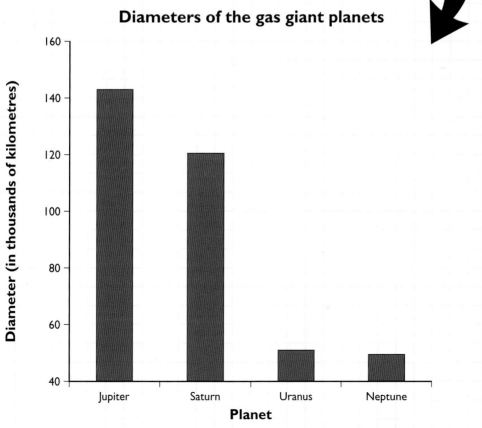

**Diameters of the gas giant planets**

Diameter (in thousands of kilometres) vs. Planet (Jupiter, Saturn, Uranus, Neptune)

The Moon, which **orbits** the Earth, shines with light reflected from the Sun. It appears to be the largest and brightest object in the night sky because it is so close to the Earth. Its average distance from Earth is 384,400 kilometres (238,855 miles), or about 30 times the diameter of the Earth.

The Moon has almost no **atmosphere**. The **craters** that cover parts of the Moon were formed when rocks hit the Moon's surface. Dark, smoother parts of the Moon, called maria, were formed when volcanoes on the Moon flooded the landscape with lava.

## Other natural satellites

The Moon is a natural **satellite**. A satellite orbits a **planet** or smaller object in space. "Natural" means it was not made by humans. Just as the Moon orbits the Earth, other natural satellites orbit other planets. Once a possible satellite is found, a group called the International Astronomical Union makes sure it is really a satellite. Then the satellite is given a number and a name.

Astronaut Buzz Aldrin left this footprint during the first Moon landing in 1969. Because the Moon has no wind or rain to wash it away, the footprint may remain there for a million years.

## Natural satellite or moon?

The natural satellites that orbit other planets are commonly called "**moons**". However, some astronomers prefer to use the name "moon" only for the Earth's natural satellite.

In 2007, the spacecraft Cassini photographed Iapetus, a strange satellite orbiting Saturn. Half of Iapetus is white, and the other half dark. The dark section has a strange ridge that makes Iapetus look something like a walnut in a shell.

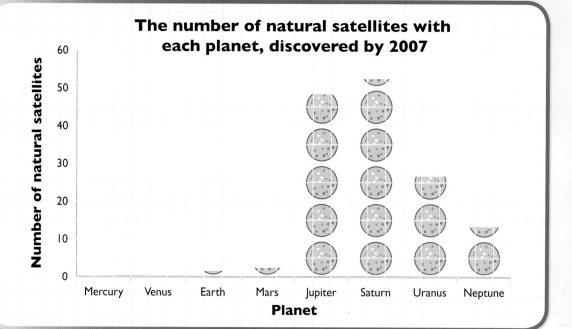

**The number of natural satellites with each planet, discovered by 2007**

This type of graph is called a pictogram. A pictogram is like a bar chart, but it uses pictures to represent **data**. Here, each picture stands for 10 natural satellites.

# DWARF PLANETS AND ASTEROIDS

Pluto is a **planet**-like object that is usually further from the Sun than Neptune. Pluto was once called a planet. However, in 2006 astronomers changed the way "planet" is defined. A planet must **orbit** a star. It must have a nearly-round shape. Pluto meets both of these requirements.

However, a planet must also have cleared the area around its orbit. This means that if there are other things near it that are also in orbit around the star, the planet must be big enough to pull the things into its **gravity**, or to move them into another orbit. Pluto has not done this. So now Pluto is called a **dwarf planet**.

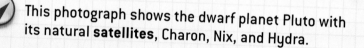

This photograph shows the dwarf planet Pluto with its natural **satellites**, Charon, Nix, and Hydra.

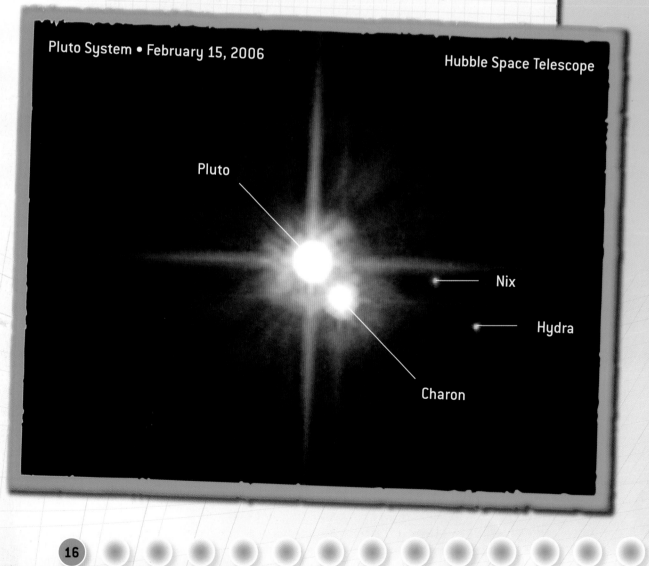

Pluto System • February 15, 2006

Hubble Space Telescope

Pluto

Nix

Hydra

Charon

As of 2007, there were two dwarf planets besides Pluto. Eris, discovered in 2005, is the largest, and is located out past Pluto's orbit. Ceres is located in the **asteroid** belt.

# Asteroids

Asteroids are small rock fragments in orbit around the Sun. Millions are found in the asteroid belt between Mars and Jupiter. Scientists believe these rocks were left over from when the **solar system** was formed billions of years ago. There are more than 200 asteroids with diameters larger than 100 kilometres (60 miles). Other asteroids are much smaller. One has a diameter of about 6 metres (20 feet).

## Making an impact

What does an asteroid have to do with dinosaurs? Many scientists believe that an asteroid hit the Earth 65 million years ago. Dust from the impact may have blocked the Sun's light. Chemicals released into the air may have changed the Earth's **climate**. Many types of life, including the dinosaurs, died out around this time.

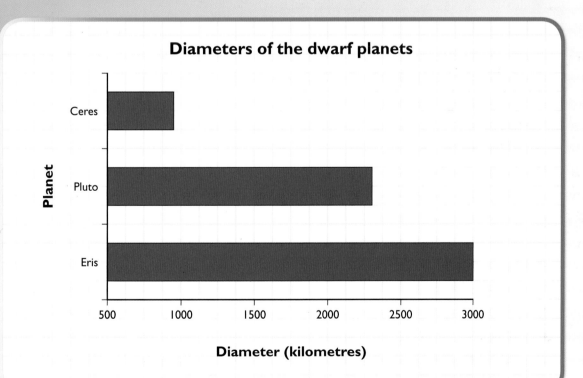

**Diameters of the dwarf planets**

This graph compares the sizes of three dwarf planets. Its bars go sideways. The same **data** could be used to make a graph with bars that go up and down.

## Comets

**Comets** travel around the Sun but are much smaller than **planets**. The main part of a comet is made up of ice, rock, dust, and frozen gases. Because of this, sometimes comets are called "dirty icebergs". Comets may have tails of gas and dust particles that stream behind them. Most comets have long, oval-shaped **orbits**. Short-period comets make the trip around the Sun in less than 200 years.

One of the most famous comets, Halley's comet, takes about 76 years to make the trip. Scientists believe short-period comets come from the Kuiper belt, a band of objects outside Neptune's orbit.

Long-period comets take 200 years or more to travel around the Sun. They may come from the Oort cloud, a huge rounded cloud of icy objects that astronomers believe surrounds the **solar system**.

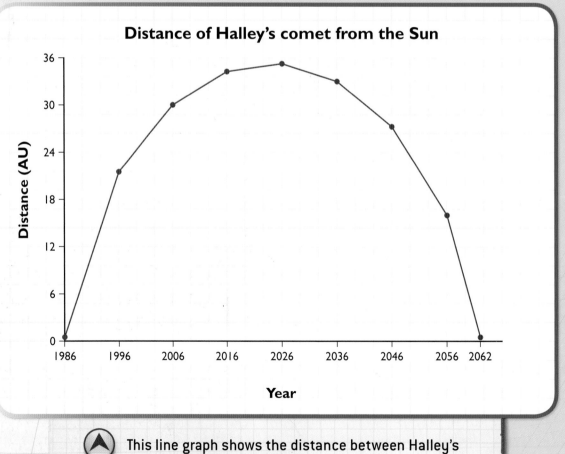

This line graph shows the distance between Halley's comet and the Sun over time.

An artist's impression of the Oort cloud.

Astronomers believe the Oort cloud stretches 30 trillion kilometres (18 trillion miles) from the Sun.

The long-period comet Hale-Bopp glows in the night sky. The comet last came near Earth in 1996–1997. It will not return to the inner solar system until around the year 4377.

# Meteors

If you see a light streak in the night sky, you are probably looking at a **meteor**, not a comet. Meteors, or "shooting stars" are bright streaks of light caused by burning chunks of material called **meteoroids**. As the meteoroid flies through Earth's **atmosphere**, it burns up. Pieces that fall to the surface of the Earth are called **meteorites**.

## Meteor showers

Sometimes the Earth passes through dust that a comet has left behind. The result is a meteor shower – a large number of meteors that come from one spot in the sky. Meteor showers are often named by the star or group of stars that they appear to come from.

Our Sun is just one of the billions of stars in the universe. The closest star to the Sun is Proxima Centauri, which is a little more than four **light years** away.

Stars are different colours, depending on their surface temperatures. Blue stars are the hottest, and red stars are the coolest. The Sun is a yellow star, with a surface temperature of about 5,770 K (see fact box).

## Floating bar charts

This is called a floating bar chart. The bars do not need to touch the bottom of the graph. The bars show the surface temperature ranges for each star colour and how the ranges compare. The temperatures are shown in kelvins (K), a measure of temperature often used by scientists.

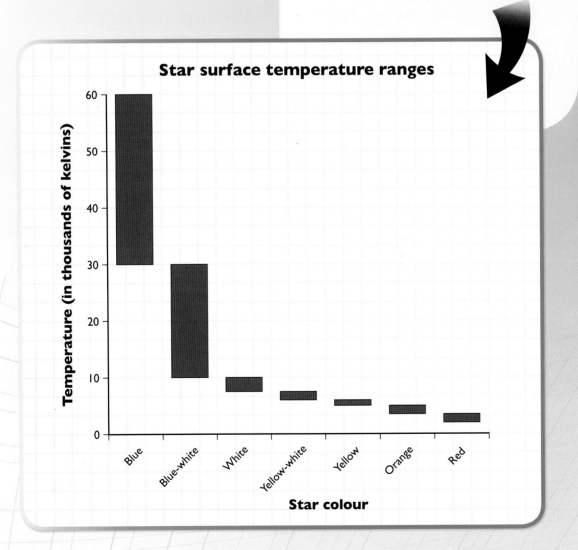

**Star surface temperature ranges**

# Pictures in the sky

A **constellation** is a pattern made by a group of stars in one part of the night sky. People in different parts of the world see different stars. The constellation Ursa Major (which means the Great Bear) can be seen in most of the northern parts of the world. Crux (the Southern Cross) can be seen from the southern parts of the Earth.

Throughout history, stars have helped sailors and other travellers navigate, or find their way. One particularly important star for navigating is Polaris. Polaris is known as the North Star, since it shows the way north.

## Looking at history

If a star is 50 light years away, its light has taken 50 years to reach Earth. When we look at that star, we are seeing it the way it looked 50 years ago. If the star changes, we won't know for 50 years! When we look at far-away stars and galaxies, we are seeing the past, not the present.

The Little Dipper is part of the constellation Ursa Minor, the Little Bear. Polaris, the North Star, is at the end of the dipper's handle.

Little Dipper

Polaris

Big Dipper

With so many stars in the universe, are there stars besides the Sun that have **planets**? The answer is yes. The first were discovered in the 1990s. As of 2007, astronomers had found 270 planets **orbiting** stars other than the Sun. As technology improves, more will surely be found.

This graph shows the number of planets outside our **solar system** that were discovered in recent years. All these planets orbit stars in the Milky Way galaxy.

## Distant galaxies

Most stars belong to **galaxies**. Astronomers believe that the Milky Way galaxy contains about 100 billion stars. But the Milky Way is just one of billions of galaxies in the universe. Some galaxies are flattened disks that have arms that spiral out like a pinwheel. Others look like balls.

A galaxy may also contain clouds of gas and dust called **nebulae**. Astronomers believe that some nebulae are "star nurseries" where new stars are made. Another type of nebula forms when a star collapses.

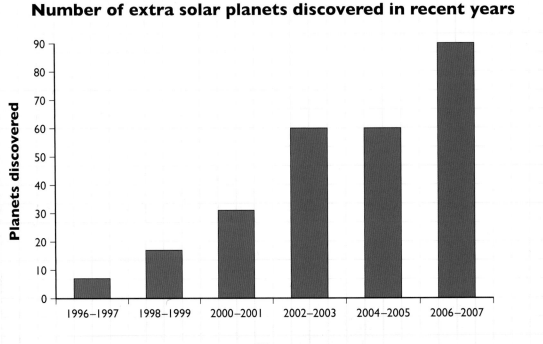

**Number of extra solar planets discovered in recent years**

⬆ This sea of glowing gases is part of the Swan Nebula, which is located about 5,500 **light years** from Earth.

## The life of a star

Stars have life cycles just as animals and plants do. Stars are born when gas and dust in a nebula pull together and begin to spin and burn. When the star grows old and its fuel begins to burn up, the outer part of the star expands. As it grows, it cools and turns red, becoming a kind of star called a red giant. Then the star either collapses or it blows up in a big explosion called a nova. Like all stars, the Sun will eventually die – but not for billions of years.

Long before **telescopes** were invented, people were studying the stars and other objects in the sky. Three thousand years ago in the city of Babylon, astronomers recorded observations about the **planet** Venus. Over two thousand years ago, the Greek astronomer Hipparchus made a list of about 1,000 stars.

## Optical telescopes

Telescopes gather information from objects in the sky. Studying space changed a great deal after telescopes were invented around 1608. No one knows for sure who made the first telescope. Hans Lippershey, a Dutch spectacle-maker, is often given credit for this.

Optical telescopes gather information in the form of light. An optical telescope uses glass lenses or mirrors to collect light from an object in the sky such as a star. It then focuses the light. When you look through the telescope's eyepiece, you see a larger picture of the object.

## Timelines

A timeline shows when certain events took place. It makes it easy to see how much time passed between events. This timeline shows when some of **astronomy's** important discoveries were made and who made them.

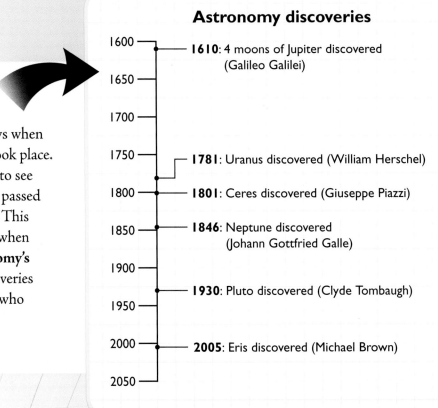

**Astronomy discoveries**

|  | |
| --- | --- |
| 1600 | **1610**: 4 moons of Jupiter discovered (Galileo Galilei) |
| 1650 | |
| 1700 | |
| 1750 | **1781**: Uranus discovered (William Herschel) |
| 1800 | **1801**: Ceres discovered (Giuseppe Piazzi) |
| 1850 | **1846**: Neptune discovered (Johann Gottfried Galle) |
| 1900 | |
| 1950 | **1930**: Pluto discovered (Clyde Tombaugh) |
| 2000 | **2005**: Eris discovered (Michael Brown) |
| 2050 | |

# Radio telescopes

Radio telescopes gather information in the form of radio waves. Objects in the sky such as stars and planets give off radio waves. These waves are the same type of waves that carry sound from a radio station through the air to your radio. Radio telescopes collect these waves and use them to create pictures of distant objects in the sky.

## The Hubble Space Telescope

As the Earth's atmosphere moves, it bends and blurs the light from stars. This makes stars seem to twinkle, even though they actually shine steadily. Telescopes on Earth must view stars through the atmosphere. The Hubble Telescope orbits above the Earth's atmosphere. This means it can take clear pictures of distant space objects.

 The Hubble Space Telescope orbits about 610 kilometres (379 miles) above the Earth.

# SPACE MISSIONS

**Telescopes** let astronomers observe space from Earth. Another way to learn about the universe is to send ships into space.

**Space probes** are spacecraft which do not carry people on board. They collect information and send it back to the Earth. Probes have been sent to observe the Moon, other **planets**, and **comets**. The Voyager 1 spacecraft is now the furthest human-made object from the Earth. It is over 15 billion kilometres (9.3 billion miles) from the Sun.

## Message to the universe

Voyager 1 and Voyager 2 each carry a gold-plated disk that contains images and sounds from Earth. If alien beings find and play the disks, they will hear music as well as greetings in many of Earth's languages. They will also see photographs of the Earth's people, animals, and landscapes.

This photograph was taken in 2004 by a space probe sent to the surface of Mars.

# Space travellers

Some space missions carry astronauts out into space. One of the most famous was the 1969 Apollo 11 mission that took astronauts to the Moon. The space shuttle currently carries astronauts into **orbit** around the Earth. Sometimes they go into space to repair the Hubble Space Telescope. The shuttle also brings people and supplies to the International Space Station, a research lab that orbits the Earth.

New spacecraft are being designed to take humans back to the Moon. There are plans to send humans to Mars sometime in the next 30 years. The information they collect will add greatly to what we know about that planet.

## Double line graphs

A double line graph is like a line graph, but it shows how two things change over time. This graph shows the distance between the Sun and each of the Voyager space probes. One line shows Voyager 1; the other shows Voyager 2.

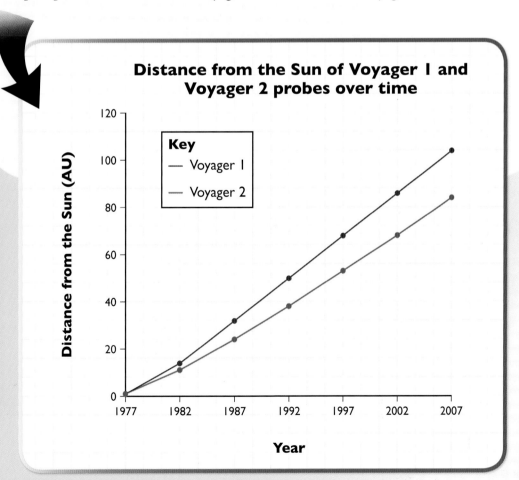

Distance from the Sun of Voyager 1 and Voyager 2 probes over time

# CHART SMARTS

**Data** is information about something. We often get important data as a mass of numbers, and it is difficult to make any sense of them. Graphs and charts are ways of displaying information visually. This helps us to see relationships and patterns in the data. Different types of graphs or charts are good for displaying different types of information.

## Pie charts

A pie chart is used to show the different parts of a whole picture. A pie chart is the best way to show how something is divided up. These charts show information as different sized portions of a circle. They can help you compare proportions. You can easily see which section is the largest "slice" of the pie.

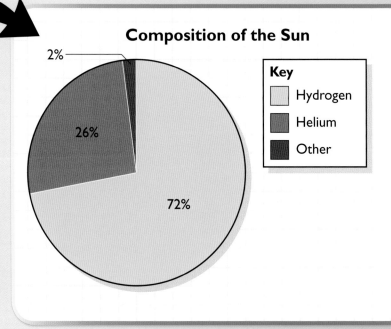

**Composition of the Sun**

2%
26%
72%

**Key**
Hydrogen
Helium
Other

## Bar charts

Bar charts are a good way to compare amounts of different things. Bar charts have a vertical **y-axis** showing the **scale**, and a horizontal **x-axis** showing the different types of information. They can show one or more different types of bars.

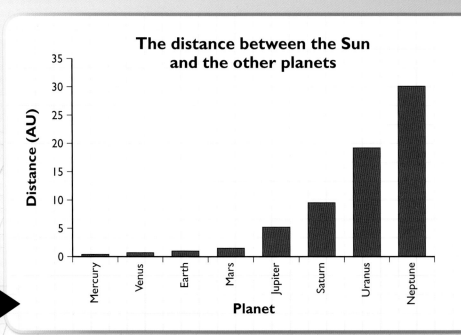

**The distance between the Sun and the other planets**

Distance (AU)

Mercury, Venus, Earth, Mars, Jupiter, Saturn, Uranus, Neptune

**Planet**

# Pictograms

A pictogram uses pictures to show data.

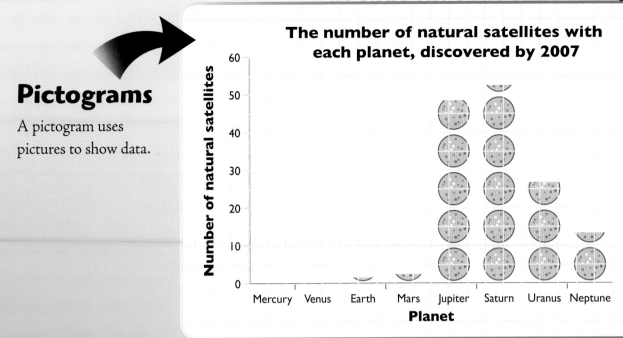

**The number of natural satellites with each planet, discovered by 2007**

# Line graphs

Line graphs use lines to join up points on a graph. They can be used to show how something changes over time. If you put several lines on one line graph, you can compare the overall pattern of several sets of data. Time, such as months or years, is usually shown on the x-axis.

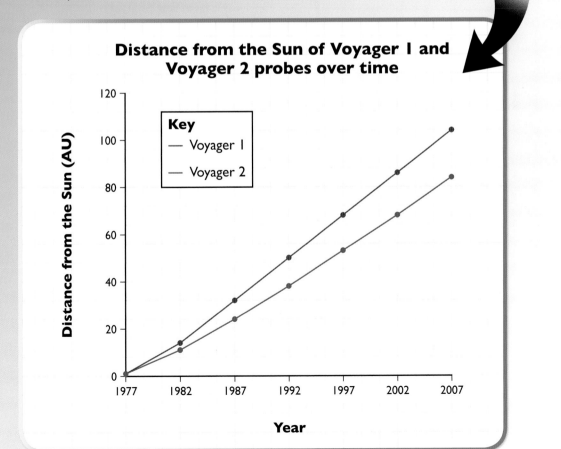

**Distance from the Sun of Voyager 1 and Voyager 2 probes over time**

Key
— Voyager 1
— Voyager 2

# GLOSSARY

**asteroid** one of the small planet-like bodies that orbit the Sun, mostly found in the area between Mars and Jupiter

**astronomical unit** the distance between the Earth and the Sun (about 150 million kilometres or 93 million miles)

**astronomy** the study of the universe

**atmosphere** layer of gases that surrounds a planet or other object

**axis** imaginary line through the centre of a planet (or other object) around which the planet rotates

**climate** the general type of weather an area has, over a period of time

**comet** icy body that travels around the Sun, often with a long, oval-shaped orbit

**constellation** group of stars in the sky that forms a pattern or picture

**crater** rounded pit found, for example, on the Moon

**data** information, often in the form of numbers

**dwarf planet** rounded object that orbits a star, but is not large enough to have cleared other objects out of its orbit

**galaxy** system of stars, dust, and gas held together by gravity

**gravity** force that pulls two objects together

**key** something that tells what symbols or colours on a graph stand for

**light year** the distance light can travel in one year

**mass** amount of matter that makes up an object

**matter** substance that makes up physical objects

**meteor** bright streak of light in the sky

**meteorite** a meteoroid that reaches the Earth

**meteoroid** piece of metal or rock travelling through space

**moon** natural satellite in orbit around a planet

**nebula** (plural = nebulae) cloud of dust and gas in space

**orbit** travel around another object

**planet** rounded body that orbits a star and has cleared the area around its orbit

**rotate** spin on an axis

**satellite** object in orbit around a larger object

**scale** relationship between the marks on a graph's axis and the measurement the graph is showing (for example, one mark on the y-axis might represent 1,000 kilometres)

**solar system** a star and the planets and other objects that orbit it

**space probe** spacecraft without a crew sent into space to collect data

**telescope** device used to observe distant objects

**x-axis** horizontal line on a graph

**y-axis** vertical line on a graph

# FURTHER INFORMATION

## Books

*Astronomy*, Kristen Lippincott (DK Publishing, 2004)

*Internet-Linked Book of Astronomy and Space*, Lisa Miles, Alastair Smith (Usborne, 2002)

*Out-of-This-World Astronomy*, Joe Rhatigan, Rain Newcomb, and Greg Doppmann (Lark Books, 2005)

## Websites

This BBC website has programmes you can watch about the night sky.
www.bbc.co.uk/science/space/spaceguide/skyatnight/proginfo.shtml

This site has photographs taken by the Hubble Space Telescope.
www.hubblesite.org

National Aeronautics and Space Administration has lots of information about the universe.
www.nasa.gov/audience/forstudents/5-8/index.html

The Royal Observatory Edinburgh has articles describing what you can see in the sky above the UK during the current month.
www.roe.ac.uk/vc/actpublic/observing/skyatnight.html

# INDEX